Quartet

Claudia La Rocco

"It just takes time"/But who has time?

—Sam Miller

Life gets complicated!

—Douglas Crimp

It's nice that people do things.

—Bill Berkson

It all turned out nicely didn't it!

—Kevin Killian

Dictation, December 21, 2019:

In the dream it's a ballet festival or a symposium. I have very fragmented memories but—there were lots of pieces that we saw, I think premieres and, I was at a bar or somewhere with, like, [crow calling], one of those restaurants that isn't very satisfying where you end up between performances. Even now I might be editorializing. But. I do remember very clearly that Christopher ... Wheeldon was [crow] I almost called him Christopher Walken [slight laughter] I was eating with Christopher and Douglas Crimp was at a nearby table and I just remember, "Oh, Douglas can, Douglas saw it, Douglas can explain it to me or he can explain myself to me if I am writing something [crow] doesn't make sense that I need help with." I woke up missing him terribly. He's not somebody I was good friends with but that sort of intimacy that develops when you go to see the same type of [sand crunching] over and over again, year after year, and you see the same people in the audience, and often they're not the people that you, you know, are closest to in the world, your partners, your best friends, your relatives. They're the people who also love this thing that you love. So, it is this sort of parallel intimacy and closeness, because you also can't sometimes share these things fully with the people you are intimate with in other ways. If you're lucky you can. Or maybe not if you're lucky, maybe you don't want to, maybe it's delicious to have this other world and place. And anyway. Yeah ... Douglas and Bill and Sam. Well, Douglas and Sam were that. Bill and Kevin were something else [wind] don't know, is there any frame for these four men, except that they all died in the span of three years? That I knew them and regarded them as sort of ... ancestors, or heroes, or elders, and miss them, although not in the way you miss the people that, you know, really hold you up in [sand], *the people you have that day-after-day intimacy with. What am I saying? I remember once an old, eminent critic told me that I would never really be serious as a dance critic unless I knew mime, was, was literal … uh, was fluent in mime, ballet mime. I remember another, older eminent critic telling me—yes, yes, they were both old white men, they were chief critics—telling me that I would have to find a way to get over to see the European festivals if I were going to be serious as a dance critic. And I suppose in a way they're both right, I mean they're right for certain types of criticism, and I don't—But I think maybe what I find, uhhh, not even irksome, just limiting about those statements is that they pres*[inaudible] *that there is only one way to be a* [crow], *or one important type of* [crow], *and I think what I love about these four men is that, they were each* [crow] *in such different* [wind] *don't think that they expected anyone to be* [crow] *although they believed absolutely in what they were doing. Um. One of them didn't even publish but was, to my mind, one of the finest poet critics I've known. So. It's the shortest day of the year. I'm collecting glass on the shore of Jones Bay for my mother for* [muffled sound]. *There are little birds in all the trees. They look like juncos; they fly like juncos and have the coloring of juncos. My eyes are not as good as they used to be.*

○

Bill Berkson, Douglas Crimp, Kevin Killian, and Sam Miller were born within thirteen years of each other, beginning with Bill in 1939, Douglas in 1944, and Sam and Kevin little more than a month apart in 1952. The four men died in a three-year span, also beginning with Bill.

I had seen him just the night before, June 15, 2016, at the 500 Club in San Francisco. A buzzing crowd was celebrating the new catalogue for a David Ireland show at the San Francisco Art Institute, co-curated by Constance Lewallen, Bill's wife; I remember Connie twirling in the middle of the action. My last glimpse of Bill, he was sandwiched between Bob Glück and Norma Cole, looking relaxed and debonair as always. Grinning that marvelous grin.

In fact, the last times (or for that matter, almost all of the times) I saw Douglas, Kevin, and Sam, the occasions involved art. Not surprising; this was the ground of our friendships. More to the point: art was life's work for each of them. As I experienced these men, all of whom I knew only in the final years of their lives, art *was* life, in an everyday sort of way: no less special for being matter of fact. In the last email I received from Kevin, a group message sent to those of us who had performed his play *Box of Rain*, which Maxe Crandall directed at The Stud, he wrote, "What an extravaganza, a golden bowl, the beginning and end of civilization…"

The beginning and end. Kevin would be gone in a little more than two weeks, on June 15, 2019, the proximity to the anniversary of Bill's death like some hideous joke. A bookend of loss in San Francisco.

Bill, along with Connie, and Kevin, along with Dodie Bellamy, hold for me the enchantment of larger than life literary and artistic traditions: Bill with his starry trajectory from New York School poets and painters to the romance of a Bolinas scene in which he and Joanne Kyger were neighbors. And Kevin, a pivotal figure in the New Narrative movement and San Francisco Poets Theater, keeper of Bay Area histories and mythologies flowing from the Berkeley Renaissance. Poets among artists, Kevin and Bill were in all the right rooms.

Douglas and Sam, meanwhile, are inextricably bound up in my New York—where I spent the first fifteen years of the millennium embedded in the downtown dance world. How many times did I sit in darkened theaters with one or both of them? How many pre- and after-show hangs, planned and happenstance? Years of casual encounters as a young, know-it-all writer before I began to understand the extent to which each laid the foundations for how I receive and understand dance and visual art; so much of it comes from movements and systems these men helped to shape, or wrote about, or both. To quote Dodie and Kevin in their introduction to *Writers Who Love Too Much: New Narrative 1977-1997*, "In time we were to see that indeed these people's lives were more interesting than ours, but self-preservation wisely hides this disparity from the young, in the name of self-esteem."

When I think of Douglas and Sam, I think of Danspace Project at St. Mark's Church; where I saw them so many times, where they were memorialized. Bill and Kevin were also honored at St. Mark's, in celebrations hosted by the Poetry Project (though I attended their San Francisco memorials, at the Art Institute and the San Francisco Museum of Modern Art).

Certain buildings form cities within cities. People who don't know each other, are not part of the same group or are adversaries even, are nonetheless united by these edifices, their ever-accumulating densities through time. It's one of the things that's impoverishing and freeing about moving to a new place, particularly when you are no longer young: the site-specific ghosts don't follow you.

Douglas' memorial was the most recent, everyone crowded into uneven rows of chairs, a temporary organism held within the sanctuary's beautiful, spare bones. He once told Danspace director Judy Hussie-Taylor that the theater was "the closest place he had to a sacred space." My mind's eye conjures the severe geometries of Emily Coates dancing Yvonne Rainer; Morgan Bassichis singing, coaxing the audience into song.

All these people in all these rooms, gathering to honor lives well lived. Public and private joined at last, however tenuously.

And all the rooms one never enters. All the people one never lets in.

The city that does not see beyond itself and its mythologies.

○

I had the idea to read each of their last books, sparked by an offhand comment from Cedar Sigo about following the books where they take you; his faith in the bread crumbs to get you through the forest stuck with me, forming a trail in and of itself.

There's an aliveness in the fragmentary, unfinished nature of these final publications (final for now; it seems impossible, for example, that Kevin's complete Amazon reviews and Douglas' Moroccan cookbook will not eventually see the light of day). They move fiercely, fitfully in the present. Bill's notebook on Frank O'Hara, published posthumously by Connie in facsimile form, the sometimes-indecipherable flow of the handwriting in keeping with the immediacy of thought. A small volume of Kevin's weekly exchanges with Dodie offered at his memorial, a joint, interrupted diary shimmering with the possibility of artifice ("…being writers, we faked the conversation," Dodie writes during the first exchange, "Origins," referring to an earlier collaboration of theirs). Douglas' not-yet-out collection of writings on dance and dance film sits in its pale blue folder on my desktop, some of the files still containing his notes, as if the author might return at any moment to make improvements. And then there is Sam's "book," which exists only in my mind, a collage of various poems he sent to me and a serial work composed as Danspace Project's writer in residence during the 2016 platform *A Body in Places*, dedicated to Eiko Otake's solo performances.

Something about the partial, arranged views offered through these windows feels right. The books are beautiful in their incompleteness. They are enough.

○

Dictation, July 19, 2020:

The way they were in the world or the way their writing is in the world [sigh] *have to pee I'm looking at the olive tree outside listening to the dull roar of the freeway. I keep not making this final recording because I don't know what the thing is that I want to say, I'm just worrying at the sentences and circling* [banging] *a freedom … the cat is racing back and forth galloping through the apartment* [breath] *uhhh* [breath] *fuh—nmmm I don't wanna swear* [banging] *a way of moving through language and experience* [long pause] *some permission given, understood through reading them—even just an idea of reading them—more than any conversations* [banging] *of course the dumb cliché it's only when you can't ask anymore that you're astonished by all the things you never asked. The cat is using the litterbox and the windchimes are going and a dog is barking* [N.B.: no evidence of any of this in the recording] *and everything outside is still and moving and this recording doesn't have any magic in it. Maybe that's the right way.* [stuffy inhale] *I keep thinking of something M. said about a pamphlet being what you can write now but isn't that what every piece of writing is? You can only do what you can do now.* [cat scratching in litterbox] *Pathos. Somebody's using a power saw* [N.B.: silence]. *Good for them.*

○

Sam was firmly of the "no conflict, no interest" school. As the revered creator and steward of various influential cultural organizations, he was the architect of numerous local, regional, and national networks underpinning the fragile ecosystem that is contemporary dance in the United States. If it's a support structure involving dance and an acronym, chances are he had a hand in it. Yet his motivations were intensely personal: as he explained it, he'd built his career around figuring out what Ralph Lemon needed, then devising a mechanism to fulfill that need. I would add a few other artists to that list of one, including Okwui Okpokwasili and Eiko—but always returning to Ralph. If you were paying attention, Sam's loves were easy to see. And if you were lucky enough to be the recipient of the achingly romantic, often elegiac poetry he wrote in and around performances, jotting words down on notecards kept in a breast pocket, these intimates surfaced again and again.

> Sitting behind R observing J—watching someone you love watching someone they love

The J here is Jimena Paz, and R can only be Ralph. The line comes from the poem-notebook Sam kept during *A Body in Places*; to my knowledge, this is his only published dance criticism. I'm not sure he even would have called it criticism.

Whether something was good or bad, whether it *worked*, is not an overriding concern in his writing. Rather, he seeks a nowness, an intensity, an attunement to the present moment. And a communion with those who shared those moments; the subject of many of the poems I received, typically after an evening out together, is some variation on "While X was ..."

He was famous for nodding off during shows—only to wake up and tell you what happened. Am I remembering or inventing that he told me once that napping through dance was not only appropriate, but called for, given how dance works on the psyche? That indeed he learned this lesson early on by attending a Merce Cunningham performance? He wouldn't describe, exactly, but he would tell you what had transpired.

The hour is very late in the Danspace writings, the fragments wreathed by what is no longer, by what could never be. Against and with these losses stands art's live, recurring moment, in which performance is forever, fleetingly, "time's rebuttal":

Catastrophe of meaning
Always hurtling toward catastrophe
Catastrophe practice
Time stops
Time must have stop
Time curved so that looking forward you can see the back of
  your own head
Capital acceleration
The autonomy of Eiko time
Mutated declensions
Singular/plural
Past/future
Timeways that send us sideways into that future

○

The first dictation: childish desire for you to feel what I felt, the glimmer of an idea that could carry me through to other ideas. A beginning, merciful relief, having married myself to a course … and then spent endless stupid hours arguing with myself about this course (Kevin: "I've made a choice, now I have to stick to it, everyone's original writing problem, now mine"). The cold fullness of a Maine winter, the air sharp and salty and intensely *clean* off the ocean, everything somehow still and moving at once. The crunch of white-gray clam and purple mussel shells turning to sand underfoot. The insistent call of crows overhead.

I remember a few days after Bill died, passing by a stranger, maybe I just didn't like his posture, the savage thought flashing "why couldn't it have been you?" My head was echoing with, amplifying, something he'd said—written?—a passing thought about the aridity of California—that its lushness was illusory. Fact taking on the strength of metaphor.

○

I wasn't surprised to learn, at his memorial, that Douglas refused to teach survey courses. In "Merce Cunningham: Dancers, Artworks, and People in the Galleries," in the October 2008 print edition of *Artforum*, he writes about Cunningham's decentralized choreography, the ways in which it challenges any illusions of a graspable whole:

> When Cunningham began making dances like this more than half a century ago, it was an enormous break with

11

existing choreographic practice, and audiences were nonplussed. Without necessarily realizing it, people had accepted the fact that choreography would make their decisions for them. In following its dictates, they were more or less assured that they wouldn't miss anything. But Cunningham no longer afforded that assurance. On the contrary, his audiences were made aware of the fact that they *would* miss things, maybe even most things. They were, in short, made aware of their inability to see totality, aware of themselves as having the limitations that a single subjectivity entails. They could see only *partially*, and they therefore had to grapple with the fact that just as Cunningham challenged the coherence of a dance, he also implicitly challenged the coherence of the spectator.

How much we can see. The limits of what we can see, and the limits in how we see.

"Dancers, Artworks, and People in the Galleries" flows from Douglas' scrupulous, joyful tracking of Cunningham's *Beacon Events* at Dia Beacon ('Events' were a site-specific mode of composition in which Cunningham arranged selections of choreography, typically excerpts from his repertory, knitting a whole from disparate parts). He quotes his *Artforum* article in his 2017 essay "Four Events that Have Led to Large Discoveries (about Merce Cunningham)," and then comments:

These limitations also turn out to be an advantage: With them Cunningham demonstrates his respect for the partiality of our individual subjectivities by allowing us the freedom to make our own meaning of what we see. Partiality is not autonomy, however; while we are partial in the sense of bringing our subjectivity to bear upon what we see, we are also partial in the sense that our subjectivity is constituted always and only in relation to what is external to us.

The critic therefore can never claim an objective or time-less meaning, because "meaning does not reside *in* a dance, waiting to be properly deciphered by its spectators. Meaning is context-specific. It is, as I said, for us to make. We bring to bear what we know, how we watch and listen, what we feel."

In Douglas' writing, desire for clarity mixes resonantly with respect for mystery. The sentences possess an integrity that I always relate to his commitment to political activism. There is a deep decency, to allow for things, oneself and other things, to be as they are. "The trouble is that our experiences are so different," he explained once after I asked for advice on a piece in which I was comparing the dances Alexei Ratmansky made for New York City Ballet and American Ballet Theatre. Trouble as in he'd be encroaching on the sovereignty of my experience.

I *was* surprised, at first, to learn that Douglas had difficulty with poetry for most of his life. So much of the dance he loved had so much—everything!—in common with poetry. But it also made sense, when I returned to his writing. Not that he isn't often direct about events from his life, but he doesn't take up space the way poet-critics do (extravagantly), remaining reserved in his subjectivities even as he underlines their existence. It's to do with shyness, perhaps—or, maybe better to say, humility.

One time he expressed to me his discomfort at being on a panel with City Ballet dancers; what would he have to contribute, compared to these artists who knew George Balanchine's choreography from the inside out? This struck me as silly—he had watched the company for decades, he knew so much!—and yet beautiful: critic as student, a generous rejoinder to the small-minded cliché of the physically brilliant, intellectually dull dancer. (I'm ashamed to say I've peddled that ugly line, parroting what I'd heard more than one newspaper critic express with devastatingly flip casualness, as though remarking on the color of the sky. So easy in hindsight to see the defense mechanism at work, earning that other cliché: the critic knows the way, but cannot drive the car.)

"Dancers, Artworks, and People in the Galleries" is one of Douglas' earliest published accounts of dance, coming decades after he established himself as a major thinker in visual art and queer theory. The article is informed by a lifelong love of dance (not only as spectator; some of his richest writing describes his devotion to disco). I wonder, now, about his reticence on the page, and his late public claiming of dance—whether either of those things was influenced by the reality of having to keep his queer, club self separate from an art world unwelcoming of homosexuality, a hostility that is hard to imagine now. I interviewed Douglas about his memoir, *Before Pictures*, when it was published in 2016, and he noted that it was only through activism that he began to bring himself into his writing: "Within my AIDS work I began to write about myself. I began to write in the first person. I began to talk about my own experience." Perhaps, early on, dance was too bound up with cherished, vulnerable sensations to seem a safe critical subject; when he did finally approach it, he did so not primarily as an expert, but as an enthusiast.

It pleases me so that Douglas turned to poetry at the very end of his life. Not in the awful, mawkish "poetry saves lives" sort of way, but just that he would be a student to the end.

○

I remember fitfully skimming a review of a book about the essay as form, I think in one of the dailies—one of those tabs that sits mostly neglected until your browser crashes. The reviewer was taking the book's author to task for misunderstanding the essay. Absurdity upon absurdity to spend any effort, let alone so much, defining and then arguing about a form we made up. I think of all the critics who have said "Well, it's not *X*," X being a stand-in for whatever Genre With A Capital G this particular critic was expecting to encounter. And then punishing the work for not being X, rather than concentrating on what it actually is. Years ago, when I interviewed Annie-B Parson and Paul Lazar about their interdisciplinary company Big Dance Theater, Annie-B succinctly addressed this problem of expectation versus experience: "We've had the right piece in the wrong theater."

○

I wrote to a friend:

I have been toying with the idea of "Four White Men: An Elegy." As a way to think through a lot of my inheritance. What to do when so much of the inheritance is ugly, but then the individuals are beautiful, or at least beloved (is there a difference)? I don't know … Maybe it's a better essay to think about instead of write.

At some point I had realized, squeamishly, that I was writing in praise of four dead white men. The inheritance: the limitation, disguised as luxury, of not immediately seeing that you are writing about four dead white men. What, if anything, to do about or with this? I like the play of that title, but it's disingenuous, glib, a way to push responsibility over to them.

My friend responded in his typically generous way: *I think any good thing to think about is worth writing about [...] any thing beautiful is also worthy of writing about. The ugly part is a given. Beauty is the sublime, the thing we argue out of how troublesome humanity really is. All the beautifully absurd Sisyphean labor and the inevitable dying that is the top of the mountain.*

His words led me back to Cynthia Carr, whom I first encountered as C. Carr, the incisive *Village Voice* chronicler of performance and visual art. Carr subsequently turned her attention close to home, in her meticulously researched book *Our Town*, investigating a white mob's

1930 lynching of two black men in Marion, Indiana—her father's hometown, where, she has learned, her grandfather was a member of the Ku Klux Klan. It is a history both deeply personal and deeply American. Carr infiltrates Klan culture, attempting to stay clear-eyed and present in the company of people with views so hateful it is easy to feel superior, to feel apart. She sees this for the trap it is: "Acting as the scapegoat for all of white racism is a Klansman's job, part of his function as the 'bad white.' He is the decoy who leads us away from looking at ourselves."

Late in the book there is a striking moment when a Wizard claims kinship with her:

> Earlier that day he'd said to me, "You're like family." [...] The fact was, I was afraid and disturbed about the ways in which I might be "one of them." I wasn't just there as a journalist, after all, but as someone with a certain inheritance to confront.

Carr spends much of *Our Town* looking at ugliness. Yet her criticality is predicated on beauty. And by beauty, I mean what is beloved: her grandfather, the town she visited as a child. I think for a lot of people the beauty is what's given, or at least the illusion of it; we have to argue out the ugliness, argue *ourselves* into the ugliness, in order to see anything at all.

○

Bill Berkson:

EVERYone has a history—the longer you live, the more you know that nothing should be forgotten.

Kevin Killian:

I feel like opening that dentist drawer one more time and looking at that candy. But it's gone.

Sam Miller:

A woman who looks up and across the sanctuary
and sees   nothing
the nothing that remains after everything is lost

except memory

Douglas Crimp:

And doubling readily becomes multiple: three characters,
four, five, and more; now this story, now that one, now
another, now that one again.

○

In "Critical Reflections," a short essay published in the November 1990 issue of *Artforum*, Bill writes:

> Verdicts and explanations call for fairly transparent and flatfooted prose styles. A critic like myself, who is interested less in systematic argument than in communicating the spontaneously dense, specific, and often paradoxical events of consciousness in the face of contemporary works, allows for occasional opacities of language. The critic who faces art's manifold dialectic head-on risks seeming to want to be abstruse when really he or she is only trying to stay true to a complex situation. I like to think that my opacities can be enjoyed for themselves, at face value, as well as for their relation to both the artist's work and the reader's sense of language in the world. Given a vivid sense, in words, of what can be seen in the work, I go as deep and as wide as I can.

He then quotes O'Hara—"We do not respond often, really, and when we do, it is as if a flashbulb went off"—describing exactly what my initial response had been upon reading Bill encapsulate what I had long felt about criticism, but hadn't quite been able to formulate: that at its core, it has nothing to do with saying whether something is good or bad, but rather with tracking the internal (consciousness), as revealed by the external (art). Bill, again:

> The truest criticism, I believe, reveals that flash, or series of flashes, in a language communicative of the intensity or force experienced in looking long and hard at art.

That electric, restless encounter. In her afterword to *A Frank O'Hara Notebook*, Connie writes, "Bill often referred to 'his sense of scatter' and 'impulsive jottings' as the first step in his process."

Writing as tracking experience. I would go further, and say that Bill's sense of scatter is the foundation of his process; not a first step on the way to something more definitive, but *the* step: *communicating the spontaneously dense, specific, and often paradoxical events of consciousness*. This deeply honed skill is what I am reading when I am reading his notebook—which, as Connie also points out, is what's on offer in the two scrapbook travelogues Bill published (*The Far Flowered Shore* and *Invisible Oligarchs*, the books of his I most cherish). Viewed in this light, the *Notebook* is not so unfinished after all.

○

Placing things next to other things. The word "parataxis." An elegant, electrifying word. Long before I learned it, I could only speak of my dread of the linear. The panic induced by news that I had been chosen to give a college-wide lecture as part of a visiting teaching artist stint. Would I have to cancel the entire residency, so as to avoid those forty-five minutes of public misery? And then, finally, slowly, stupidly, the question: how is it I could love giving a poetry reading, love the sensuousness of having my words received by others, while a lecture, essentially the same transaction, engendered fear and loathing? What if the lecture thought it was a poem? What would happen then?

○

Dictation, May 17, 2020:

I'm talking about this idea of inheritance, and beauty and ugliness, and [wind] *how to not, how to not have to compartmentalize. What's beautiful to me about what Carr's doing, what's important about it, is that she is not looking away. She's looking. And I think it's very easy in fact to use writing as a way to look away. To camouflage, right. It's what the guy says in* Ad Astra, *that you're exploring but in fact, no, the exploration* [oak titmouse] *is just a means of escape, and* [breathing]. *To not use criticism and rhetoric as a means of escaping from being clear-eyed, which is so, which is different to me from, uhh, the shame and blame game and ah, what is it, that thing you do when you are seeking to be validated, signaling, virtue signaling* [sigh] *something about the loneliness and impoverishment of white contemporary culture, or whenever there's sort of a white cultural group, how often it's ugly.* [airplane]. *By not looking at the ugliness, we don't really get to hold the beauty. Avoidance protects and destroys. The luxury is the limitation.*

○

"Dancers, Artworks, and People in the Galleries," the title of Douglas' *Artforum* piece, is a play on "Dancers, Buildings and People in the Streets," a 1965 essay by the poet and critic Edwin Denby, who originally wrote it as a lecture for dance students at the Juilliard School; its subject is no less than seeing, as understood through the lens of dance criticism.

More than a few people credited Denby with helping them learn how to truly see, an anecdotal-historical snippet I latched onto when Judy asked me to be the guest curator for a Danspace platform in 2015. Douglas of course makes reference to the Denby essay-as-lecture in his *Artforum* article, and I chose to use verbatim Denby's title for the Danspace project, which aimed among other things to frame the critic as connector rather than judge.

Here is one of Denby's sentences:

> At the beginning of what I said today I talked about one sort of seeing, namely a kind that leads to recognizing on stage and inside yourself an echo of some personal, original excitement you already know.

Douglas is one of the contributors to the catalogue for my platform, and Bill was one of the readers in the opening event, a tribute to Denby co-presented with the Poetry Project. Sam was then on the Danspace board, and often in attendance at the platform; was he there that night? Yes. I search my email and find this, in response to my thank you note to him:

> I couldn't miss one of your opening nights, what a great spirit there was in the room!

> and a lovely Denby quote "instinctive behavior in complex situations"

I wonder what, if any, connection Kevin had to Denby; surely there must have been some thread. I turn to the search engine and find something Kevin wrote in 2009 for Open Space, a meditation on John Giorno titled "The Institution":

> He had pioneered the "Dial-a-Poem" service, where you picked up a phone—heavy old rotary phones then, most of them black—slid the little hole around a standard dial, like picking a safe—how slow and balletic it seems now, compared to the punching the numbers we've come to know (or now touching the screen, the ultimate in affordances). Anyhow a recorded voice would come on—did they change every day? If I remember right, some days were "live" days when Edwin Denby or Jim Carroll or [Robert] Creeley or Muriel Rukeyser would be answering the phone themselves. Now when I want some of that same thrill I pick a day I know Michael McClure will be out of town on a gig, and then I dial his home number and his answering machine has him reading one of his own, loveliest poems.

○

Several years ago I was in Texas, giving a lecture on criticism. I was trying to form some sort of grand connection between criticality and democracy:

> Far from telling us what to think, real criticism proposes *how* one might start thinking about the questions that inevitably lurk behind our gut responses. These lurkers remain invisible unless we pull them out and examine them; criticism is one such examining table, in a society that often prefers going with its gut.

My prime model for how to begin examining the questions behind our responses was Cynthia Carr. I pointed to an interview I did with her, in which she discussed how much time she spent in her early days as a performance critic simply teaching herself how to see; she wanted to understand the why behind her strong reaction to this new work, to be clear-eyed in the face of artists who were either ignored, dismissed, or despised by most of her male colleagues at the *Voice*. (These same colleagues reacted to Carr's coverage with childish sexism no less shocking for its predictability). "I would take profuse notes," she told me, "and then I would go home and transcribe the entire tape; I have a notebook filled with these transcriptions and drawings of the costumes and everything. It's about an inch thick, typed single-spaced on both sides. I was trying to teach myself how to really observe."

I made the argument that being "an insightful critic of subversive American art" uniquely prepared Carr to do the work of *Our Town*. But now I think that's a leap, and a self-congratulatory one at that, a claim by association to something I haven't yet earned. It's all too easy to perform self-exploration as a writer—or, worse still, fool yourself into believing you're doing that work.

"I was a lunar astronaut for Space Com for thirty-one years," Colonel Thomas Pruitt tells Major Roy McBride in *Ad Astra*, a film that troubles the notion of the lone, heroic white man while ultimately celebrating just that.

> And I came to the realization out there, a voyage of exploration can be used for something as simple as escape. I'm telling

you this, Roy, because we have to hold out the possibility that your father may be hiding from us.

Commander H. Clifford McBride is, if not exactly hiding, deep in space. "We are a dying breed," he unrepentantly tells Roy on the battle-scarred space station where his son has tracked him, a trail of bodies and long-suffering ladies behind them. Only Roy returns home, armored in the newfound awareness that separates him from his murderous zealot of a father. Commander McBride is the decoy who leads him, and therefore us, away from looking at ourselves.

○

"I hardly know a thing about him, the best time to plunge into something don't you think?"

This was from almost the first email Kevin sent me, in June of 2015, inviting me to visit a Kurt Seligmann retrospective at the Weinstein Gallery in San Francisco. I was living a trial period in Oakland that spring, on the cusp of deciding I would move across the country.

Where others might see disparate points, Kevin saw constellations vast in scope—intimately related, yes, to a sense of scatter, but not quite the same thing. This way of working should not be confused with how a dilettante operates: he knew his subjects deeply, and knew, too, that research doesn't necessarily follow predictable vectors.

We got a great parking spot and, buoyed by karma, approached the gallery with a careless jouissance—only to be jolted by the sign that says the space is open only from Monday till Friday. Confronted with such a sign, who doesn't give the door a little push anyway? And surprise, it opened to our touch like something from Alfred Hitchcock's *Spellbound*.

There is the path, and there is the way you choose to go; later you see, or perhaps it is pointed out to you, that this as well is the path.

I suppose you could resist getting caught up in Kevin's enthusiasms, but why would you want to? Beyond the myriad pleasures to be had in following the critic's roving eye is the important realization that everything is connected, or could be, so long as you remain alive to chance encounters. Did I care about Seligmann? No, to my detriment. And yet there I was, no doubt wanting to appear sophisticated, drifting along, peering into these strange surrealist works. I still can feel my physical registering, while standing in front of a photograph of a fancifully dressed ballerina, that I actually already knew this Swiss-American artist, glancingly: he designed the costumes for the 1946 Balanchine ballet *The Four Temperaments*, costumes Balanchine would soon reject in favor of the stripped-down practice clothes that would come to define his modernist aesthetic. Give the door a little push.

You see Kevin's honed ability to rove in his published exchanges with Dodie. You see it as well in her writing; I remember the exhilaration of reading *When the Sick Rule the World*, the writing flirting with driving too fast to make the curve, making the curve. Kevin's writing is similarly full of virtuosic lines. So much of its power resides in its sweep, in the tragic undergirding and activist sensibilities that give shape and meaning to linguistic spectacle.

I don't think I ever asked him about dance; certainly, I don't remember us talking about it. Another lost opportunity. Even when not written explicitly for the stage, his writing performs. It *moves*. Until it doesn't. You've been wandering through the city and then jogging, now stopping to look at a window display, now sprinting into the surrounding fields, until you find yourself at—over—the cliff's edge, suspended, the ground suddenly far below. In *Kevin and Dodie*, he writes, "Both of us have a sense of ending and that's one of our strengths as writers and thinkers." This is true. But endings depend on what has come before—the kineticism of Kevin's criticism allows the stillness of his shimmering endings to reverberate out.

> I'm hysterical today, let my hysteria explode inside the great white apex of Ed Dorn's heart.

Everything is admissible, provided you can get away with it; and you always can get away with it. Even, maybe especially, when you don't. When you dead end, double back, get lost, redirect.

The Dorn line concludes 1995's "Open Letter to the Editors of *Apex of the M*," a terrible and glorious and terribly, gloriously funny letter in which Kevin tries to understand how the magazine editors justify publishing the poetry of the man responsible for the "AIDS Awards for Poetic Idiocy," a homophobic cruelty doled out by Dorn's *Rolling Stock* journal in the 1980s. One of the recipients was Steve Abbott, a New Narrative founder who would die from the virus a few years after receiving the loathsome award.

Except the line doesn't conclude things, not really. Kevin troubles over the letter, bringing it to a conference five years later, and then bringing it up in the chapbook with Dodie, where he writes,

> in the early days of AIDS, when none of us knew what a mammoth tragedy it would become, I stopped myself several times from making the kind of flip joke about AIDS that I later crucified Tom Clark and Ed Dorn for making. I was furious with them because it was so close. It might have been me who had given out to lesser poets the AIDS Award for Poetic Idiocy. This haunts me.

○

It occurs to me that being a general critic is like teaching a survey course. The illusion of neutrality, of a linear story to tell. How much you have to take in in order to tell that story. How much you have to keep out.

We value empathy elsewhere in our society, but the thumbs up, thumbs down review, the idea of criticality, critical distance... as if you might get to a hill where you see everything clearly, your breathing calms, and you can just pronounce... No. Another trap. One that precludes the possibility that the richest criticism might lie in paying attention to—in answering to—what you love.

○

Bill writes about art as the escape hatch.

> Try it this way: I come from a level of the urban upper middle-class which, for males, breeds extraordinary dullness and repression. A level from which, to live, one must go down, or up, or out. I was not good at down. Up meant aristocratic pretensions [...] or dandyism. Out meant crazy, drugs, or maybe, Art.

Of course one could say that it's precisely because Bill was a handsome straight white man who came from the urban upper middle-class that he had the freedom to venture out. And yet and still. I do not want to flatten the complexity of these individuals along identity vectors, even as I do not want to ignore the ways in which these vectors are part of the complexity. And it isn't even quite that; I'm not a biographer, I don't want to chart lives, draw conclusions. I want to learn lessons.

Imagine the privilege of imagination, Sam writes.

In describing how she envisions the Danspace platforms, Judy often talks about how best to productively trouble history even as you celebrate it. I like this formulation very much. Of course it is the present we trouble, not the past; the past only (only!) troubles us.

○

A few months after Kevin died, I was at a performance, and Connie and Dodie were also in attendance. I remember looking up and seeing them across the room, their backs to me, holding hands. I flashed on something Connie had expressed in the wake of Bill's death, her disgust with being in the widow's club. How easily women are reduced to sidekicks. But also … there was something so childlike and private about this moment, between these two formidable individuals. Hansel and Gretel in the woods. The experiences one can only share with fellow travelers.

○

I don't want to claim anything universal for or about any of them. What they believed or didn't. That they didn't try to control or determine how others behaved … perhaps they did. They were always only generous with me; more to the point, their writing is only ever that. People can make the day bigger or they can make it smaller.

○

Just because something is worth thinking about, worth looking at, doesn't mean you are willing, or even know how, to do it.

○

I am sitting under the redwood tree that the horrid neighbor has hacked into, the tree that maintains its sovereignty, nonetheless. Thinking through how I would/will/did write the essay. The day is going, going, gone. Soon, there will be bats. Have there always been bats, or am I only now noticing them?

"The dance everyone did there was called the spastic. It's one of the only dances I could never learn to do." *(Douglas)*

"And at that point it was like: oh okay, this is more about atmospherics and particular experiences, not some kind of family tree." *(Sam)*

"Words have a separate system, an integrity of
their own, and they can't be used to formulate
a representation of Life." *(Kevin)*

"I am not proposing a theory, a poetics here so much as just letting you know some of the strands of thought that have been on my mind for some time, and maybe to help myself draw them together." *(Bill)*

Acknowledgements

Quartet draws primarily on Bill Berkson's *A Frank O'Hara Notebook* (no place press, 2019); Douglas Crimp's *Dance Dance Film Essays* (Dancing Foxes Press, forthcoming); Dodie Bellamy and Kevin Killian's *Kevin and Dodie* (published in conjunction with Kevin Killian: Celebration held at SFMOMA on August 25, 2019); and Sam Miller's writings at https://danspaceproject.org/tag/sam-miller/.

In addition to those publications, private correspondence, and previously acknowledged works, quotes are taken from:

Kevin Killian's "Sex Writing and the New Narrative" in *Writers Who Love Too Much: New Narrative Writing 1977-1997* (Nighboat Books, 2017) and "A Less Shadowed Place" on SFMOMA's Open Space platform; Douglas Crimp and Claudia La Rocco's "The Pleasures of Promiscuity: An Evening with Douglas Crimp," on Open Space; Cynthia Carr and Claudia La Rocco's "East of Eden" on Artforum.com; Claudia La Rocco's "Husband and Wife, Marrying Art Forms" in *The New York Times*; Pat Nolan's "Don't Mess with Bill: An Appreciation of Bill Berkson," on Otoliths; Douglas Crimp's *Before Pictures* (Dancing Foxes Press and University of Chicago Press, 2016); Bill Berkson's *Invisible Oligarchs* (UDP, 2016); Sam Miller in "Conversation" from *A Body in Places* (Danspace Project, 2016)

Thanks:

To the dancers in New York, and the musicians in the Bay Area, for teaching me how to listen and how to look.

To Dodie Bellamy, Cynthia Carr, and Constance Lewallen, for the writings.

To Judy Hussie-Taylor, for holding space.

To Ugly Duckling Presse for asking me to write something I wouldn't otherwise have written; to Paige Parsons for several deft edits, and in particular to Matvei Yankelevich for being so generous and thoughtful.

To Karen Kelly and Barbara Schröder of Dancing Foxes Press, for an early glimpse of Douglas' dance and dance film anthology. To Connie, for answering pestering questions. To DiverseWorks, for a previous invitation to muddle through what's so important about Cynthia Carr.

To Silas Riener, Rashaun Mitchell, Evan Kleekamp, Cedar Sigo & Ralph Lemon for consultations and encouragements. To Cedar, and to Okwui Okpokwasili, for words and kindness. To Diana Cage & the ACC, for making everything better. To Phillip Greenlief, for time and space.

To Bill, Douglas, Kevin, and Sam.

Apologies:

To Christopher Wheeldon. And Christopher Walken.

2020 Pamphlet Series
ISBN 978-1-946433-52-7
First Edition, First Printing
Edition of 1,000

Ugly Duckling Presse
The Old American Can Factory
232 Third Street, #E-303
Brooklyn, NY 11215
uglyducklingpresse.org

Distributed in the USA by SPD/Small Press Distribution
Distributed in the UK by Inpress Books

Series design by chuck kuan and Sarah Lawson
Typeset by Don't Look Now!
Type is New Century Schoolbook
Cover paper and flyleaf from French Paper Co.
Printed offset and bound at McNaughton & Gunn
Flyleaf printed letterpress at Ugly Duckling Presse

This publication is made possible, in part, by support from the
New York State Council on the Arts, a state agency. This project
is supported by the Robert Rauschenberg Foundation.

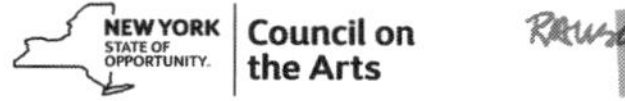